BEAUTY OF THOUGHTS

BEAUTY OF THOUGHTS

FATEMA ABBAS VALI

PAPER TOWNS
PUBLISHERS

PAPER TOWNS
PUBLISHERS

First published by
Papertowns Publishers
72, Vishwanath Dham Colony,
Niwaru Road, Jhotwara,
Jaipur, 302012

Beauty of thoughts

ISBN Print Book - 978-81-951287-6-1

Cover Design by Aditi Shah
Instagram Id: @the.book.story
aditicshah01@gmail.com

Accept your life, your life
will accept you.

Let everything that has breath,
praise for it to the lord. Today
just be thankful for life.

You can do it

Life itself is a big chapter that is written by you only not others.

At the end of the end day, remind yourself that you did the best you could do today and that is good enough.

You can do it

Basic Mantra: Living our best life today.

Life never provides any warranty or guarantee it can only provide opportunities and Possibilities.

You can do it

Faith is the greatest asset
in the world.

Hatred can never end with hate
but with love.

You can do it

Bad temper can spoil many things
so keep it in control.

If you feel like apologizing to anybody just
do it then and there without any delay.

You can do it

In any relationship it is important to build a bridge of understanding.

You can only give guidance to others but they have to walk the path on their own.

Your work will matter to the world not your opinion.

Have a desire to see other person's perspective.

You can do it

Small steps in the right direction can turn out to be the greatest step of your life.

Have a strong will power so that no one can suppress you easily.

Whatever we put into the universe
will come back to us.

Two things prevent us from happiness; living in the past and comparing your life with others.

You can do it

Sometimes it is better to do it now than postpone or that day will never come.

There's no such thing as being too busy. It's only the matter of priority.

You can do it

Stress rises from ignoring mistakes
and their consequences.

Everyone is born with a million dollar idea.
What is not present in everyone is the will and
work ethic to execute that idea.

You can do it

Judge people by their principles not by your own.

Implementation and transformation is more important than just collecting information.

You can do it

Sometimes a little diplomacy is useful.

You need to control your tone while communicating. Communication is not just words but how are they expressed?

You can do it

Life is not a problem to be solved
but a reality to be experienced.

If you are thankful for what you have you'll end up having more. If you concentrate on what you don't, you will never ever have enough.

Earn money according to your need
not your greed.

In the end you won't remember people with just beautiful face but with beautiful soul who will create space in your mind as well as your heart.

You can do it

Never discourage anyone who continuously makes progress however slow.

Focus on your long term goals, it will show results soon.

You can do it

Don't worry God is always on time even
if you miss yours.

Be prepared for every level of your life
because every level requires a different you.

You can do it

Doubt and overthinking kills more dreams
than failure ever will.

Never regret things that once
made you smile.

Negativity is basically laziness. It takes a lot of hard work to remain positive in your daily activities and it always pays off.

You are free to choose but you are not free from its consequences. So be prepared.

You can do it

Your mind is a powerful tool. Fill it with positive thoughts and your life will begin to change.

Choose the best options of what is available. If not then do your best with what is available.

You can do it

Don't judge your decision based on the advice of those who don't have to deal with the results.

When you truly want something then go after it without any disbelief; the universe will make it happen.

You can do it

Knowledge is abundant.
Try learning something new everyday.

Your surroundings won't affect you much
if you stay focused on your work.

Everything happens for the good.
Sooner or later it will be seen.

When we change ourselves for the better,
our life follows suit.

You can do it

You don't get the life you dream of.
You get what you work for.

Success doesn't come to you overnight
but with consistent work.

It is important to take risks but more important is to trust on its results and keep working on it.

Relationships are like electricity.
Wrong connection will give you shocks but the right ones will light up your life.

Don't be scared to sacrifice the good for something great.

The best revenge is moving on.

You can do it

Forgive but don't forget to save yourself from repeating previous mistakes.

Controlling your anger for a moment can save you ample of time from regret.

You can do it

Make your comeback stronger
than the setback.

Be good in real life
not just on social media.

Attitude is what differs ordeal
from adventure.

Don't try to control the situation around you.
Try to control how you deal with it.

You can do it

Take your passion as God's gift sent to you specifically with certain purpose.

Don't burn your opportunities for a temporary comfort.

Every lie we tell incurs a debt on truth.
Sooner or later the debt is paid off.

You are a unique lock and only you have the power, the skill, the strength, the ability to create a unique key to open your door to success.

You can do it

Sometimes feelings are better expressed
with action than with words.

When you feel low,
use an elevator and rise higher.

You can do it

Everyone is useful in their area.
Be good to all and they will help you as and when needed in Life.

Everything is possible if you want it to happen.
No matter who is there for you or against you.

You can do it

Laughing in general may lengthen our life.
Laughing at others won't.

Everyone has there opinions.
You cannot fit in all of them.

You can do it

What we think determines what we become eventually. So to change their lives, one needs to stretch their minds.

Do not upset with people or situation. Both are powerless without your reaction.

You can do it

If you are dedicated enough and working on your goals there is no need for extra push. The vision itself pulls you.

The greatest enemy of knowledge isn't ignorance. It's the illusion of knowledge. Be Conscious.

You can do it

Do not work on two different things at the same time. Finish one of them soon enough to get onto other one.

Decide what kind of life you actually want and then say NO to everything else that isn't part of that decision.

You can do it

You are already destined for something and maybe you desire it too. But your choices decide whether you get there sooner or later.

An apology is simply manipulation if you repeat previous mistakes.

Upgrade yourself everyday compared to yesterday.

A smile is your charm and beauty.
Keep smiling
Start your day with a smile and spread happiness.

You can do it

Don't spoil your plans by telling it to everyone.
Just pleasantly surprise them with
your Actions.

The struggle you are going through today
gives you necessary strength for tomorrow.

You can do it

A person who feels appreciated will always do more than what is expected.

Do not break anyone's trust. It's the most expensive thing in the world. You won't be able to regain it easily.

You can do it

Someone somewhere is praying for the things you take for granted.

Creativity is a natural extension of your enthusiasm.

Be the reason for someone's smile today.

Continuous improvement is better than delayed perfection.

Don't stress yourself on missing your targets. Keep going and you will reach there.

Be a love digger not a gold digger.

Change is the only constant in life
and up gradation-adaptation is the only way
to survive that.

Funniest people are the smartest ones.
Because it's not easy to make someone laugh.

You can do it

Over-addiction to anything leads
to a trap you can't escape.

God will either heal your heart or heal the situation. Either way it will work out.

If your mind is beautiful on the inside,
it doesn't matter what's on the outside.

Single word or sentence uttered wrongly
can lead to thousand difficulties.
Think before you speak.

You can do it

You always get to learn from your mistakes.

Never lose the ones who helped you
in difficult times.
Keeping them always by your side will help
you grow further.

Prayers are one's biggest strength.

Cooperation can be seen when you give other people's ideas and feelings the same importance as your own.

You can do it

Be hearty in your approbation and
lavish in your praise.

Everyone has a different path to walk on.
So don't judge others without walking
in their shoes.

Before taking any step carefully review the situation and remember your principles.

Be aware of things you do.
Lack of awareness can tarnish your image.

You can do it

Don't wait for things to get better. Learn to be happy with everyday events before you lose the moment and run out of time.

You will never be criticized by someone who is ahead of you. The ones who are running behind will try to pull you back by discouraging.

Being original is never right or wrong.
Don't be afraid of being yourself.

Misunderstanding is never ended by baseless arguments but by facts and cooperation.

You can do it

Everything is worthless
if you are unhappy.

In a relationship keep emphasising good
things and avoid pinpointing bad ones.

He who treads softly goes far.

Perfect relationship is not the one where you never fight with each other. It's the one where you bounce back to normal.

You can do it

Make your pain your strength
not your weakness.

Even if you lose everything,
you will have your family by your side.

Keep peace in your mind, love in your heart and happiness in your relationship.

When you are going through something hard and wonder where God is, remember the teacher is always quiet during a test.

You can do it

Shine bright not light.

Don't give up, the beginning is always the hardest.

You can do it

Be the person who spread kindness
in the world of anger and negativity.

Life doesn't happen by itself.
We have to make it happen.

If you are in the dark just remember that you have the glow in you to shine in the dark like a star.

The body receives what the mind believes.

A mother's heart is a benchmark of love.

Learn how to be a confident individual.

You can do it

Today's bread is the only bread you can possibly eat. So think of today first.

Make less friends but build that friendship so strong that the world remembers.

You can do it

No one can drag you down without your consent. Don't allow that negativity to get into your mind.

Look around. You have a lot to cheer about rather than to complain.

You can do it

Evil exists due to human ego and
Good exists due to divine light.

Never change your goals, the means
to reach that goal can change.

Be careful to manage between personal life and professional one. Going always after money can be harmful.

Always be thankful for your job; the people you are working for. Because it's them who are enabling you to pay for your food and bills everyday.

You can do it

Don't show-off to go broke one day.

Miracles are possible in your life too once you start realizing about the magical powers of your subconscious mind and use them.

Look within. There's a gold mine inside you.

Keep on putting in the work until the day breaks and the shadow flees away.

The universe keeps the balance always
in the end. Come what may.

Never waste your time thinking
about people you don't like.

You can do it

Try and accomplish all you want
with what you have.
Or someone else more courageous will.

Don't be disappointed in bad times. If you keep on putting the work, time will take it's course and change as per your will.

You can do it

Success and Excuses cannot go hand in hand.
If you want to succeed stop hiding
behind Excuses.

Think about your mistakes before talking
about others.

Be a good listener and try to read
between the lines.
Their lies all the answers you would need.

Every saint has a past.
Every devil has a future ahead.

You can do it

Success has many fathers.
Defeat is an orphan.

Every phase of life teaches you a lesson.
You just need the willingness to learn from it.

No material possession is as worthy as happiness.

We don't own the Earth, we belong to it just like other living beings. We must try to share it fairly with other wildlife. Because we cannot survive without them.

You can do it

Damaging a person's dignity is a crime.

Train your mind to remain calm
in any adverse situation.

Praise is like a warmth of sunlight
to the human spirit.

Use encouragement while pointing out a mistake to make the fault seem easy to correct.

You can do it

Do not promise what you cannot deliver.

Keep on making mistakes and learn continuously. You will taste success one day.

Sometimes you need to disconnect
a little to reconnect.

It's always scary before every
new beginning.

You can do it

If you can't change your fate,
change your attitude.

Always remember that you are unique.

Nobody is perfect. Everyone makes mistakes. Correcting them sooner or later distinguishes one from another.

Your father is the strongest among all family members who can hide tears behind his smile.

You can do it

What we do for ourselves dies with us.
What we do for others remains forever.

You are brave than you believe, stronger
than you seem, smarter than you think.

You can do it

Knowing is not enough.
One should put things into application.

You are what comes out of your mouth.
So choose your words wisely.

You can do it

The most valuable treasure in the world
is a heart filled with love.

Life gets much better when you stop
taking things personally.

You can do it

Small changes add up to huge results.

There's always light at the end of the tunnel.

You can do it

Six best healers in life:

1. Sunlight, 2. Water, 3.Healthy diet,
4. Air, 5. Exercise, 6. Rest

The greatest gift you can give someone is your time and attention.

You can do it

Life is about giving love and care
without expecting it in return.
Because it's about feeling not deal.

Stop overthinking things before it
breaks you.

You can do it

Stop for a moment and take out time to thank God for what you have.

Stop worrying and start living.

Where there are gentlemen, there is a dialogue; but where there are fools, there is a conflict. Choose your company wisely.

Life is like a maths equation. In order to gain the most, one has to find out how to convert the negatives into positives.

You can do it

The moment you accept responsibility
for everything good or bad in your life
is the moment you get the control of it.

Nothing ever goes away until it teaches us
what we need to know.

Learn to manage your time to manage your work.

Occupy your time with work to leave no place for negativity.

You can do it

Hard times don't change people,
it just reveals the real face of people.

Everyday may not be completely fine,
but there's always some good in everyday.

Blowing out someone else's candle
doesn't make your smile brighter.

The best feeling in the world is to know
that your parents are happy and smiling
because of You.

You can do it

One peck of sand at a time. One task at a time.

Instead of looking at one reason to quit, think about 1000 reasons why you started it.
It will help you motivate to reach your goal.

You can do it

Feelings are like visitors. Pamper the good one's more and let the bad ones leave sooner.

Direction is so much more important than the speed. Many are just running faster in circles, reaching nowhere.

Something needs to be left behind
to go ahead.

You only fail when you stop trying.

Never let your fear decide your future.

You can't enter next chapter of your life if you keep revisiting previous chapters again and again.

You can do it

Better to live a few years as a tiger than to spend the whole life as a sheep.

If someone is stupid enough to leave you be smart enough to let them and move on.

You can do it

If everything feels like an uphill struggle just imagine the view from top.

It's an awesome feeling to achieve something others said you cannot.

Be your own sunshine. Self motivation is a great source of energy.

Focus on your task otherwise the flare to continue will be lost.

You can do it

Make your life simple but significant.

Your dream doesn't have an expiry date.
Take a deep breath and try again.

You can do it

Don't always trust your eyes.
Even salt looks like sugar.

Create such an identity that even if someone spoke ill of you no one will believe it.

You can do it

Creativity involves breaking out of established patterns by looking at things from a different Perspective.

Someone who takes time to listen to people at their lowest is rare and should be valued.

You can do it

Sometimes your heart takes time
to accept what your mind already knows.

If you want respect you give respect.

When people are trying to bring you down it means you are above them.

Sometimes being selfish isn't so bad.

You can do it

Any change is difficult in the beginning, a little messy in between but gorgeous in the end.

The Sun teaches us two valuable lessons:

1) Even the greatest falls, with time

2) If you fall, you can rise back to the top.

When life gives you hard time, counter back
by showing how strong you are
to sustain those hardships.

If each one of us thinks about others the way
one does for themselves,
the world would be a better place to live.

Life and Time are the two biggest teachers
of the world.

Power of God already resides in you
in the form of body strength, sense, breath,
and emotion.

Three main ingredients of success are ambition, hard work and faith.

Be stubborn on your vision but flexible on its details.

You can do it

Your perspective to the situation decides the path ahead and towards your destiny.

Yes and No, very small words with huge impact. So many things go wrong because one says No too early or Yes too late.

Learn to sit back and observe.
Not everything deserves a reaction.

Your sibling is like a lens through
which you can see your childhood.

You can do it

Happiest people don't have the best of everything. They make the best out everything.

If you don't receive the same efforts you put into a relationship or friendship. It's time to rethink about it and let go of it if needed.

The price of discipline is certainly less than the pain of regret.

The answer is always NO to the things you don't ask for.

You can do it

If you can't do any good for someone,
you don't have any right to do bad either.

Irony is that smart people sound crazy to
dumb ones they are working under.

Be an Eagle not a Parrot. Speak only what's significant and reach greater heights.

Sometimes it's just a missing piece that a person needs.

You can do it

One should not always remain in the survival phase and try to enter the growth phase asap.

Loneliness and Solitude both connected to being alone. While loneliness is being in pain, solitude is being glorified when alone.

You can do it

To know your true image in society,
make your neighbours angry.

The only disability in life is a bad attitude.

You can do it

Your style speaks volumes about your
personality without uttering
a single word from your mouth.

Remember there are two words in the world
that will open a lot of doors for you:
Push and Pull.

You can do it

By plucking the petals of a flower, you are only losing the beauty of a flower. Embrace the beauty of a person with care and love.

There is no Age limit to learning new things.

You can do it

Cut off all the toxic people from your life ruthlessly. There will be immense rise in your happiness with such a small step.

What lies behind us and what lies ahead of us is of least importance compared to what lies besides us or with us.

Being glamorous is not a crime.
Not being your true self is.

We fail, we break, we retry and fail again. Later on we learn we heal, we rise back and overcome the failure with success.

You can do it

Always look into nature.
There lies all answers to all the problems
if you look in the right place.

Whatever you decide to do just make sure
it gives you happiness.

You can do it

A creative man is motivated by the desire to achieve more, not by desire to beat others.

Life isn't about waiting for the storm to pass. It's about learning to dance in the rain.

You can do it

Temple, Church, Mosque, Gurudwara are different addresses of the same resident.

God always pours love in one way or the other. We just have to look for it.

You can do it

Memories of childhood were the dreams that you lived.

Keep working until their ignorance turns into acceptance.

You can do it

Laziness will not take you to your goals. Working consistently towards them will.

Patience and positivity are a person's real strength.

Learning from your mistakes counts as experience which leads to perfection.

Promises lose their worth when broken. Be careful when you make one.

You can do it

Don't bother about other people's
opinions for you.
They change according to their
likes and dislikes.

Never ignore a person who cares for you.
You will lose a diamond while being busy
collecting stones.

Best way to deal with haters is
to keep calm and stay classy.

Trust no one until you have eaten much salt
with him or her.

You can do it

When the past calls, let it go to voicemail.
It has got nothing new to say.

Divine treat includes holy talks
and holy minds.

Learn to appreciate what you have before it's gone.

Hope is what gives one the strength to step out and try.

Never take a shortcut to success in life.
Taking a long route gives
opportunity to take more experience.

Money should be used and people
should be loved not the other way round.

You can do it

Everyday is a gift and that's why it's called present.

Laugh as much as you breathe and love as long as you live.

You can do it

God's plan is like a movie. All the good and
bad things are arranged
to have a happy ending.

Win as if you were used to it.
Lose as if it's for a change.

Whatever is for your good will come to you on it's time. Don't be impatient about it.

Live without depending, love without pretending, listen without defending, speak without offending.

You can do it

Ambition is the first step to success.
Second step is action.

If others are jealous of you,
you are doing things right.

You can do it

Good friends, good books and
a sleepy conscience: This is an ideal life.

Having a best friend with the same
mental disorder is a blessing.

You can do it

Nothing in the world is ever completely wrong.
Even a stopped clock is right twice a day.

Sometimes you will never know the value
of a moment until it becomes a memory.

When God blesses you financially, raise your standard of giving.

If you want your life to be a comfortable journey, reduce the luggage of expectations.

You can do it

Gender doesn't define your rights.

Crying isn't a weakness. Your birth is an indication that it's just a sign of being alive.

You can do it

Impossible only means that you haven't found it's solution yet.

Childhood is the most beautiful of all phases of life.

You can do it

Enthusiasm is the greatest asset you can possess. It can take you further than money, power or influence.

Anger is a condition in which your tongue works faster than the mind.

Every second spent with the
family members is worth it.
Even if it goes on for days
in a single stretch.

Happiness is not about acquiring it
but to be able to feel it too.

Forget the things that hurt you.
Remember the ones that make you happy.
Forget the trouble that passed away.
Accept the blessing that comes your way.

Trust is like a piece of paper.
Once crumpled it's never the same.

Beauty without intelligence
is a masterpiece painted on a Napkin.

If you want to go ahead fast, walk alone.
If you want to go far, go together.

You can do it

The greatest lesson of life is to know
that sometimes even fools are right.

Don't make a permanent decision
based on a temporary emotion.

Life is like riding a bike. It's impossible to maintain balance without standing still.

If you are alive,
there is purpose left for you.

One's life shrinks or expands based on the level of their courage.

Life has no remote control which you can change while sitting at one place.

You need to get up and work
for it to get better.

You will meet two kinds of people in your life:
One who will bring you up and another
who will bring you down. In the end you will
thank both of them.

You may take several decisions in life
but the basic principle
behind them should remain the same.

Feel grateful and be thankful to mother nature
everyday for all the life essentials it provides.

Love yourself everyday. Because in the end it's one and only you alone.

A good life is one where you smile often, dream big, laugh a lot and realise how blessed you are for what you have.

You can do it

A person's true nature is revealed
by what he/she is behind your back.

When you can't reach your goals;
change the path, not your goals.

First to apologise is the bravest. First to forgive is the kindest. First to forget is the happiest.

It hurts a lot when you trust someone blindly and the person proves that you are actually blind.

You can do it

A family is like a tree with family members like branches going in different directions but the support system like roots remains the same.

No words can describe parents and their efforts. They are priceless.

Love your enemies ten times more than
they hate you. Spread happiness.

Your wealth and status doesn't make you good. Your kindness and character does.

You can do it

The problem with the world order is that smart people are full of doubts while dumb people are full of confidence.

Depression is your mind telling you it's tired of playing the character you are trying to be.

Count your blessings not your troubles.

Life isn't judged by how many breaths you take but how many moment take your breath away.

Life has many ways of testing a person's will. Either by having nothing happen at all or by having everything happen all at once.

Everything in life is temporary. Either good or bad, it won't last forever.

Your life is your message to the world.
Make sure it's inspiring.

Honesty is a power that very few people
can handle.

You can do it

Good people do not need laws to tell them to act responsibly while bad ones always find a way around the law.

Avoiding certain people to protect your emotional health is not weakness, its wisdom.

You can do it

Relationships never die a natural death. They are murdered by ego, disrespect, selfishness or disloyalty.

Family and friends are hidden treasures. Seek them out and enjoy their riches.

You can do it

It's not important to have a huge friend list on facebook and whatsapp. But having that friend is necessary who can read your face and ask what's up.

One good book is equal to 100 friends while having a good friend is equal to a library.

May you be filled with wonder,
touched by peace.

If you realise how powerful your thoughts are,
you would never think of a negative thought.

Challenges always come to prepare you for the great things that are about to come your way.

Crying is like breathing. The more you hold in, the more uncomfortable you get.

If you wish strongly, have courage and endurance; you will get to the summit of your dream.

Three very important things that you can give it to others as well as keep it for yourself are: Your words, smile and grateful heart.

You can do it

Be strong enough to control your anger before it controls you.

A goal without a plan is just a wish.

You can do it

Just because something is tough to get doesn't mean you should give up. Instead you should put more effort and work harder to achieve it.

Some people always want to see you go down. Use that to reach even greater heights.

You can do it

Limits are just a state of mind.
You can always push yourself to do better.

You only live once. But if you do it right,
once is enough.

Before going to sleep every night forgive everyone and sleep with a clean heart.

You run the day or the day runs you.

You can do it

Never dream about success.
Work for it.

One day all those late nights and
early mornings will pay off.

You can do it

If you want to fly, give up everything
that weighs you down.

Before you say something, think how you'd feel
if someone said it to you.

If God brings you to it.
You will get past it too.

The more you sweat in practice.
The less you bleed in battle.

You can do it

Life has got two rules:

1. Never quit

2. Never forget rule #1

If it doesn't challenge you,
it's not good for you.

You can do it

We must take adventures in order to know where we truly belong.

When someone does something wrong, don't forget all the things they did right.

The flower doesn't think of competing with the flower next to it. It just blooms.

Our attitude towards others determines their attitude towards us.

You can do it

It never gets easier.
You just get stronger.

Define your own life.
Don't let others write the script.

You can do it

There is a certain happiness in being silly and ridiculous.

Life isn't about finding yourself.
Life is about making yourself.

You can do it

Making one person smile can change the world. Maybe not the whole world, but their world.

Every storm in life is followed by a rainbow.

You can do it

Keep smiling and one day life will get tired of upsetting you.

We blame society but forget that we are society.

You can do it

Respect yourself enough to walk away from anything that no longer serves you, grows you or makes you happy.

At the end of the day, the only question one should ask is... Did I love enough? Did I laugh enough? Did I make a difference?

Deep conversations with the right people are priceless.

Decision defines destiny.

You can do it

Your friends should motivate and inspire you. Your circle should be well rounded and supportive. Keep it tight. Quality over quantity always.

If everyone is moving forward together, then success takes care of itself.

The only person you are destined to
become is the person you decide to be.

Do not promise when you're happy.
Do not respond when you are angry.
Do not when you're sad.

You can do it

We all have problems. The way we solve them is what makes us different.

Today is the last blank page of 365 days you've lived so far. End writing a good one.

Acknowledgements

I wish to express my deep gratitude and sincere thanks to Mr. Sultan Dalal, Mrs. Shehnaz Valiudin Vali, Miss. Zahrunisa Safri, & Mr. Abbas Vajiuddin Vali. Thank you so much for invaluable guidance, constant encouragement, & immense motivation.

I can't forget to offer my sincere thanks to my parents Mrs. Benazir Abbas Vali & Mr. Abbas Vajiuddin Vali, my family, friends, mentors who always gave me valuable advice and support.

I also want to thank my readers who will stick with my book through the whole period.

I want to thank everyone, especially those who have taught me good lessons and said anything positive to me. I heard it and it meant something.

I have also written the famous quotes of famous personalities. Whom I admire. I want to honour them by putting their quote in my book, Thank you for spreading positivity.

Lastly and more importantly, I want to thank the publishing house, Paper Towns, to show trust and belief in a 15 year old girl.